THE NATSARIM
-HOMESCHOOL PLANNER-
BY SCRIBBLES & SCRIPTURES

Welcome to the Natsarim Homeschool Planner!

This planner was designed to support your family's journey through a faith-based, Torah-centered homeschool year. Inside, you'll find tools to help you organize lessons, plan for biblical feast days, set spiritual and academic goals, and track your progress—all while keeping YHWH at the center of your home.
We pray this planner inspires joy, discipline, and creativity in your homeschool journey as you build a foundation rooted in the Word.
May it be a blessing to you and your family throughout the year!

Shalom and blessings,
The Scribbles & Scriptures Team

THE YEAR AHEAD

Family Mission Statement:

ACADEMIC GOALS BY SUBJECT

Math:

Reading:

Writing:

Science:

History:

Bible:

Electives:

BOOK LIST FOR THE YEAR

THE YEAR AHEAD

Words for the year:

UNIT STUDY IDEAS BY SUBJECT - THEMES / TOPICS

Math:

Reading:

Writing:

Science:

History:

Bible:

Electives:

FIELD TRIP IDEAS FOR THE YEAR

OUR GOALS THIS YEAR

Academic:

Biblical:

Behavioral:

Creative:

Social:

OUR GOALS THIS YEAR

Physical:

Faith Based:

Yearly Assessment Goals:

Social:

OUR GOALS THIS MONTH

Month: _______________________________________

Academic:

Spiritual:

Social / Family:

Personal Growth:

Planning / Organizing:

Giving:

Field Trips This Month:

Month: ______________________________________

sunday	monday	tuesday	wednesday

<table>
<tr><td>thursday</td><td>friday</td><td>saturday</td><td>**Torah Portions**</td></tr>
<tr><td></td><td></td><td></td><td>Torah:

Haftorah:

Besora:</td></tr>
<tr><td></td><td></td><td></td><td>Torah:

Haftorah:

Besora:</td></tr>
<tr><td></td><td></td><td></td><td>Torah:

Haftorah:

Besora:</td></tr>
<tr><td></td><td></td><td></td><td>Torah:

Haftorah:

Besora:</td></tr>
<tr><td></td><td></td><td></td><td>Torah:

Haftorah:

Besora:</td></tr>
</table>

word of the week:	weekly gratitude:

SCHOOL   SPIRITUAL   MEMORY WORK

THIS WEEKS MENU

S	M	T	W	T	F	
B	B	B	B	B	B	B
L	L	L	L	L	L	L
D	D	D	D	D	D	D

SUNDAY ____/____

MONDAY ____/____

TUESDAY ____/____

WEDNESDAY ____/____

THURSDAY ____/____

FRIDAY ____/____

SATURDAY ____/____

WEEK OF: _______________________________________

| word of the week: | weekly gratitude: |

SCHOOL

SPIRITUAL

MEMORY WORK

THIS WEEKS MENU

S	M	T	W	T	F
B	B	B	B	B	B	B
L	L	L	L	L	L	L
D	D	D	D	D	D	D

| SUNDAY ___/___ |

| MONDAY ___/___ |

| TUESDAY ___/___ |

| WEDNESDAY ___/___ |

| THURSDAY ___/___ |

| FRIDAY ___/___ |

| SATURDAY ___/___ |

week of: ___________________________________

word of the week:

weekly gratitude:

SCHOOL

SPIRITUAL

MEMORY WORK

THIS WEEKS MENU

S	M	T	W	T	F	
B	B	B	B	B	B	B
L	L	L	L	L	L	L
D	D	D	D	D	D	D

SUNDAY ___/___

MONDAY ___/___

TUESDAY ___/___

WEDNESDAY ___/___

THURSDAY ___/___

FRIDAY ___/___

SATURDAY ___/___

week of: _______________

<table>
<tr><td>word of the week:</td><td>weekly gratitude:</td></tr>
</table>

SCHOOL	SPIRITUAL	MEMORY WORK

THIS WEEKS MENU

S	M	T	W	T	F	
B	B	B	B	B	B	B
L	L	L	L	L	L	L
D	D	D	D	D	D	D

| SUNDAY ___/___ |

| MONDAY ___/___ |

| TUESDAY ___/___ |

| WEDNESDAY ___/___ |

| THURSDAY ___/___ |

| FRIDAY ___/___ |

| SATURDAY ___/___ |

week of: _______________________________

| word of the week: | weekly gratitude: |

SCHOOL

SPIRITUAL

MEMORY WORK

THIS WEEKS MENU

S	M	T	W	T	F
B	B	B	B	B	B	B
L	L	L	L	L	L	L
D	D	D	D	D	D	D

| SUNDAY ___/___ |
| MONDAY ___/___ |
| TUESDAY ___/___ |
| WEDNESDAY ___/___ |
| THURSDAY ___/___ |
| FRIDAY ___/___ |
| SATURDAY ___/___ |

OUR GOALS THIS MONTH

Month: _______________________________________

Academic:

Spiritual:

Social / Family:

Personal Growth:

Planning / Organizing:

Giving:

Field Trips This Month:

Month: ____

sunday	monday	tuesday	wednesday

<table>
<tr><td>thursday</td><td>friday</td><td>saturday</td></tr>
</table>

Torah Portions

Torah:

Haftorah:

Besora:

Torah:

Haftorah:

Besora:

Torah:

Haftorah:

Besora:

Torah:

Haftorah:

Besora:

Torah:

Haftorah:

Besora:

week of: _______________________

word of the week:

weekly gratitude:

SCHOOL

SPIRITUAL

MEMORY WORK

THIS WEEKS MENU

S	M	T	W	T	F	
B	B	B	B	B	B	B
L	L	L	L	L	L	L
D	D	D	D	D	D	D

SUNDAY ____/____

MONDAY ____/____

TUESDAY ____/____

WEDNESDAY ____/____

THURSDAY ____/____

FRIDAY ____/____

SATURDAY ____/____

Week Of: _______________________

word of the week:

weekly gratitude:

SCHOOL

SPIRITUAL

MEMORY WORK

THIS WEEKS MENU

S	M	T	W	T	F	
B	B	B	B	B	B	B
L	L	L	L	L	L	L
D	D	D	D	D	D	D

SUNDAY ___/___
MONDAY ___/___
TUESDAY ___/___
WEDNESDAY ___/___
THURSDAY ___/___
FRIDAY ___/___
SATURDAY ___/___

week of: _______________________________________

| word of the week: | weekly gratitude: |

SCHOOL   SPIRITUAL   MEMORY WORK

THIS WEEKS MENU

	S	M	T	W	T	F
B						
L						
D						

SUNDAY ____/____

MONDAY ____/____

TUESDAY ____/____

WEDNESDAY ____/____

THURSDAY ____/____

FRIDAY ____/____

SATURDAY ____/____

week of: _______________________________

<table>
<tr><td>word of the week:</td><td>weekly gratitude:</td></tr>
</table>

SCHOOL

SPIRITUAL

MEMORY WORK

THIS WEEKS MENU

S	M	T	W	T	F	
B	B	B	B	B	B	B
L	L	L	L	L	L	L
D	D	D	D	D	D	D

SUNDAY ____/____

MONDAY ____/____

TUESDAY ____/____

WEDNESDAY ____/____

THURSDAY ____/____

FRIDAY ____/____

SATURDAY ____/____

week of: _______________________

word of the week:	weekly gratitude:

SCHOOL

SPIRITUAL

MEMORY WORK

THIS WEEKS MENU

S	M	T	W	T	F	
B	B	B	B	B	B	B
L	L	L	L	L	L	L
D	D	D	D	D	D	D

SUNDAY ____/____

MONDAY ____/____

TUESDAY ____/____

WEDNESDAY ____/____

THURSDAY ____/____

FRIDAY ____/____

SATURDAY ____/____

OUR GOALS THIS MONTH

Month: _______________________________

Academic:

Spiritual:

Social / Family:

Personal Growth:

Planning / Organizing:

Giving:

Field Trips This Month:

Month: _______________________________

sunday	monday	tuesday	wednesday

<table>
<tr><td>thursday</td><td>friday</td><td>saturday</td><td>**Torah Portions**</td></tr>
<tr><td></td><td></td><td></td><td>Torah:

Haftorah:

Besora:</td></tr>
<tr><td></td><td></td><td></td><td>Torah:

Haftorah:

Besora:</td></tr>
<tr><td></td><td></td><td></td><td>Torah:

Haftorah:

Besora:</td></tr>
<tr><td></td><td></td><td></td><td>Torah:

Haftorah:

Besora:</td></tr>
<tr><td></td><td></td><td></td><td>Torah:

Haftorah:

Besora:</td></tr>
</table>

week of: _______________________________

<table>
<tr><td>word of the week:</td><td>weekly gratitude:</td></tr>
</table>

SCHOOL

SPIRITUAL

MEMORY WORK

THIS WEEKS MENU

S	M	T	W	T	F
B	B	B	B	B	B	B
L	L	L	L	L	L	L
D	D	D	D	D	D	D

SUNDAY ___/___

MONDAY ___/___

TUESDAY ___/___

WEDNESDAY ___/___

THURSDAY ___/___

FRIDAY ___/___

SATURDAY ___/___

week of: _______________

<table>
<tr><td>word of the week:</td><td>weekly gratitude:</td></tr>
</table>

SCHOOL   SPIRITUAL   MEMORY WORK

THIS WEEKS MENU

S	M	T	W	T	F	
B	B	B	B	B	B	B
L	L	L	L	L	L	L
D	D	D	D	D	D	D

SUNDAY ____/____

MONDAY ____/____

TUESDAY ____/____

WEDNESDAY ____/____

THURSDAY ____/____

FRIDAY ____/____

SATURDAY ____/____

week of: _______________________

<table>
<tr><td>word of the week:</td><td>weekly gratitude:</td></tr>
</table>

SCHOOL   SPIRITUAL   MEMORY WORK

THIS WEEKS MENU

S	M	T	W	T	F	
B	B	B	B	B	B	B
L	L	L	L	L	L	L
D	D	D	D	D	D	D

SUNDAY ___/___

MONDAY ___/___

TUESDAY ___/___

WEDNESDAY ___/___

THURSDAY ___/___

FRIDAY ___/___

SATURDAY ___/___

WeeK of: _______________________________________

word of the week:

weekly gratitude:

SCHOOL

SPIRITUAL

MEMORY WORK

THIS WEEKS MENU

S	M	T	W	T	F	
B	B	B	B	B	B	B
L	L	L	L	L	L	L
D	D	D	D	D	D	D

SUNDAY ____/____

MONDAY ____/____

TUESDAY ____/____

WEDNESDAY ____/____

THURSDAY ____/____

FRIDAY ____/____

SATURDAY ____/____

word of the week:	weekly gratitude:

SCHOOL

SPIRITUAL

MEMORY WORK

THIS WEEKS MENU

S	M	T	W	T	F	
B	B	B	B	B	B	B
L	L	L	L	L	L	L
D	D	D	D	D	D	D

SUNDAY ____/____

MONDAY ____/____

TUESDAY ____/____

WEDNESDAY ____/____

THURSDAY ____/____

FRIDAY ____/____

SATURDAY ____/____

OUR GOALS THIS MONTH

Month: _______________________________

Academic:

Spiritual:

Social / Family:

Personal Growth:

Planning / Organizing:

Giving:

Field Trips This Month:

Month: ____

sunday	monday	tuesday	wednesday

<table>
<tr><td>thursday</td><td>friday</td><td>saturday</td><td>**Torah Portions**</td></tr>
</table>

thursday	friday	saturday

Torah Portions

Torah:

Haftorah:

Besora:

Torah:

Haftorah:

Besora:

Torah:

Haftorah:

Besora:

Torah:

Haftorah:

Besora:

Torah:

Haftorah:

Besora:

week of: ______________________________________

word of the week:

weekly gratitude:

SCHOOL

SPIRITUAL

MEMORY WORK

THIS WEEKS MENU

	S	M	T	W	T	F
B						
L						
D						

| SUNDAY ___/___ |
| MONDAY ___/___ |
| TUESDAY ___/___ |
| WEDNESDAY ___/___ |
| THURSDAY ___/___ |
| FRIDAY ___/___ |
| SATURDAY ___/___ |

week of: _______________________________

| word of the week: | weekly gratitude: |

SCHOOL

SPIRITUAL

MEMORY WORK

THIS WEEKS MENU

S	M	T	W	T	F	
B	B	B	B	B	B	B
L	L	L	L	L	L	L
D	D	D	D	D	D	D

SUNDAY ___/___

MONDAY ___/___

TUESDAY ___/___

WEDNESDAY ___/___

THURSDAY ___/___

FRIDAY ___/___

SATURDAY ___/___

week of: _______________________

word of the week:

weekly gratitude:

SCHOOL

SPIRITUAL

MEMORY WORK

THIS WEEKS MENU

S	M	T	W	T	F	
B	B	B	B	B	B	B
L	L	L	L	L	L	L
D	D	D	D	D	D	D

SUNDAY ____/____

MONDAY ____/____

TUESDAY ____/____

WEDNESDAY ____/____

THURSDAY ____/____

FRIDAY ____/____

SATURDAY ____/____

week of: _______________________

word of the week:	weekly gratitude:

SCHOOL

SPIRITUAL

MEMORY WORK

THIS WEEKS MENU

S	M	T	W	T	F
B	B	B	B	B	B	B
L	L	L	L	L	L	L
D	D	D	D	D	D	D

SUNDAY ____/____

MONDAY ____/____

TUESDAY ____/____

WEDNESDAY ____/____

THURSDAY ____/____

FRIDAY ____/____

SATURDAY ____/____

week of: ________________________

word of the week:	weekly gratitude:

SCHOOL

SPIRITUAL

MEMORY WORK

THIS WEEKS MENU

S	M	T	W	T	F	
B	B	B	B	B	B	B
L	L	L	L	L	L	L
D	D	D	D	D	D	D

SUNDAY ____/____

MONDAY ____/____

TUESDAY ____/____

WEDNESDAY ____/____

THURSDAY ____/____

FRIDAY ____/____

SATURDAY ____/____

OUR GOALS THIS MONTH

Month: ___________________________

Academic:

Spiritual:

Social / Family:

Personal Growth:

Planning / Organizing:

Giving:

Field Trips This Month:

Month: _______________________________________

sunday	monday	tuesday	wednesday

<table>
<tr><td>thursday</td><td>friday</td><td>saturday</td><td>**Torah Portions**</td></tr>
</table>

thursday	friday	saturday	Torah Portions
			Torah: Haftorah: Besora:
			Torah: Haftorah: Besora:
			Torah: Haftorah: Besora:
			Torah: Haftorah: Besora:
			Torah: Haftorah: Besora:

week of: _______________________

word of the week:	weekly gratitude:

SCHOOL   SPIRITUAL   MEMORY WORK

THIS WEEKS MENU

S	M	T	W	T	F	
B	B	B	B	B	B	B
L	L	L	L	L	L	L
D	D	D	D	D	D	D

SUNDAY ____/____

MONDAY ____/____

TUESDAY ____/____

WEDNESDAY ____/____

THURSDAY ____/____

FRIDAY ____/____

SATURDAY ____/____

week of: _______________________

<table>
<tr><td>word of the week:</td><td>weekly gratitude:</td></tr>
</table>

SCHOOL   SPIRITUAL   MEMORY WORK

THIS WEEKS MENU

S	M	T	W	T	F	
B	B	B	B	B	B	B
L	L	L	L	L	L	L
D	D	D	D	D	D	D

SUNDAY ____/____

MONDAY ____/____

TUESDAY ____/____

WEDNESDAY ____/____

THURSDAY ____/____

FRIDAY ____/____

SATURDAY ____/____

week of: _______________________

<table>
<tr><td>word of the week:</td><td>weekly gratitude:</td></tr>
</table>

SCHOOL   SPIRITUAL   MEMORY WORK

THIS WEEKS MENU

S	M	T	W	T	F
B	B	B	B	B	B	B
L	L	L	L	L	L	L
D	D	D	D	D	D	D

SUNDAY ___/___

MONDAY ___/___

TUESDAY ___/___

WEDNESDAY ___/___

THURSDAY ___/___

FRIDAY ___/___

SATURDAY ___/___

week of: _______________________________

word of the week:	weekly gratitude:

SCHOOL

SPIRITUAL

MEMORY WORK

THIS WEEKS MENU

S	M	T	W	T	F	
B	B	B	B	B	B	B
L	L	L	L	L	L	L
D	D	D	D	D	D	D

SUNDAY ___/___

MONDAY ___/___

TUESDAY ___/___

WEDNESDAY ___/___

THURSDAY ___/___

FRIDAY ___/___

SATURDAY ___/___

week of: _______________________

<table>
<tr><td>word of the week:</td><td>weekly gratitude:</td></tr>
</table>

SCHOOL	SPIRITUAL	MEMORY WORK

THIS WEEKS MENU

S	M	T	W	T	F	
B	B	B	B	B	B	B
L	L	L	L	L	L	L
D	D	D	D	D	D	D

SUNDAY ___/___

MONDAY ___/___

TUESDAY ___/___

WEDNESDAY ___/___

THURSDAY ___/___

FRIDAY ___/___

SATURDAY ___/___

OUR GOALS THIS MONTH

Month: ______________________________

Academic:

Spiritual:

Social / Family:

Personal Growth:

Planning / Organizing:

Giving:

Field Trips This Month:

sunday	monday	tuesday	wednesday

thursday	friday	saturday

Torah:

Haftorah:

Besora:

Torah:

Haftorah:

Besora:

Torah:

Haftorah:

Besora:

Torah:

Haftorah:

Besora:

Torah:

Haftorah:

Besora:

week of: _______________________________

word of the week:	weekly gratitude:

SCHOOL

SPIRITUAL

MEMORY WORK

THIS WEEKS MENU

S	M	T	W	T	F	
B	B	B	B	B	B	B
L	L	L	L	L	L	L
D	D	D	D	D	D	D

| SUNDAY ___/___ |
| MONDAY ___/___ |
| TUESDAY ___/___ |
| WEDNESDAY ___/___ |
| THURSDAY ___/___ |
| FRIDAY ___/___ |
| SATURDAY ___/___ |

week of: ________________________

<table>
<tr><td>word of the week:</td><td>weekly gratitude:</td></tr>
</table>

SCHOOL	SPIRITUAL	MEMORY WORK

THIS WEEKS MENU

S	M	T	W	T	F	
B	B	B	B	B	B	B
L	L	L	L	L	L	L
D	D	D	D	D	D	D

SUNDAY ____/____

MONDAY ____/____

TUESDAY ____/____

WEDNESDAY ____/____

THURSDAY ____/____

FRIDAY ____/____

SATURDAY ____/____

week of: _______________________________

<table>
<tr><td>word of the week:</td><td>weekly gratitude:</td></tr>
</table>

SCHOOL   SPIRITUAL   MEMORY WORK

THIS WEEKS MENU

S	M	T	W	T	F	
B	B	B	B	B	B	B
L	L	L	L	L	L	L
D	D	D	D	D	D	D

SUNDAY ____/____

MONDAY ____/____

TUESDAY ____/____

WEDNESDAY ____/____

THURSDAY ____/____

FRIDAY ____/____

SATURDAY ____/____

week of: _______________________________

word of the week:	weekly gratitude:

SCHOOL

SPIRITUAL

MEMORY WORK

THIS WEEKS MENU

	S	M	T	W	T	F
B						
L						
D						

SUNDAY ___/___

MONDAY ___/___

TUESDAY ___/___

WEDNESDAY ___/___

THURSDAY ___/___

FRIDAY ___/___

SATURDAY ___/___

week of: _________________________________

<table>
<tr><td>word of the week:</td><td>weekly gratitude:</td></tr>
</table>

SCHOOL　　　　SPIRITUAL　　　　MEMORY WORK

THIS WEEKS MENU

S	M	T	W	T	F	
B	B	B	B	B	B	B
L	L	L	L	L	L	L
D	D	D	D	D	D	D

SUNDAY ____/____

MONDAY ____/____

TUESDAY ____/____

WEDNESDAY ____/____

THURSDAY ____/____

FRIDAY ____/____

SATURDAY ____/____

OUR GOALS THIS MONTH

Month: _______________________________

Academic:

Spiritual:

Social / Family:

Personal Growth:

Planning / Organizing:

Giving:

Field Trips This Month:

Month: ____

sunday	monday	tuesday	wednesday

<table>
<tr><th>thursday</th><th>friday</th><th>saturday</th></tr>
</table>

Torah Portions

Torah:

Haftorah:

Besora:

Torah:

Haftorah:

Besora:

Torah:

Haftorah:

Besora:

Torah:

Haftorah:

Besora:

Torah:

Haftorah:

Besora:

week of: _______________________________

<table>
<tr><td>word of the week:</td><td>weekly gratitude:</td></tr>
</table>

SCHOOL	SPIRITUAL	MEMORY WORK

THIS WEEKS MENU

S	M	T	W	T	F	
B	B	B	B	B	B	B
L	L	L	L	L	L	L
D	D	D	D	D	D	D

SUNDAY ___/___

MONDAY ___/___

TUESDAY ___/___

WEDNESDAY ___/___

THURSDAY ___/___

FRIDAY ___/___

SATURDAY ___/___

week of: _______________

<table>
<tr><td>word of the week:</td><td>weekly gratitude:</td></tr>
</table>

SCHOOL	SPIRITUAL	MEMORY WORK

THIS WEEKS MENU

	S	M	T	W	T	F	
B	B	B	B	B	B	B	
L	L	L	L	L	L	L	
D	D	D	D	D	D	D	

SUNDAY ____/____

MONDAY ____/____

TUESDAY ____/____

WEDNESDAY ____/____

THURSDAY ____/____

FRIDAY ____/____

SATURDAY ____/____

week of: _______________________________

| word of the week: | weekly gratitude: |

SCHOOL   SPIRITUAL   MEMORY WORK

THIS WEEKS MENU

S	M	T	W	T	F	
B	B	B	B	B	B	B
L	L	L	L	L	L	L
D	D	D	D	D	D	D

SUNDAY ____/____

MONDAY ____/____

TUESDAY ____/____

WEDNESDAY ____/____

THURSDAY ____/____

FRIDAY ____/____

SATURDAY ____/____

week of: _______________

<table>
<tr><td>word of the week:</td><td>weekly gratitude:</td></tr>
</table>

SCHOOL	SPIRITUAL	MEMORY WORK

THIS WEEKS MENU

S	M	T	W	T	F	
B	B	B	B	B	B	B
L	L	L	L	L	L	L
D	D	D	D	D	D	D

SUNDAY ____/____

MONDAY ____/____

TUESDAY ____/____

WEDNESDAY ____/____

THURSDAY ____/____

FRIDAY ____/____

SATURDAY ____/____

week of: _______________________

<table>
<tr><td>word of the week:</td><td>weekly gratitude:</td></tr>
</table>

SCHOOL

SPIRITUAL

MEMORY WORK

THIS WEEKS MENU

S	M	T	W	T	F	
B	B	B	B	B	B	B
L	L	L	L	L	L	L
D	D	D	D	D	D	D

SUNDAY ___/___

MONDAY ___/___

TUESDAY ___/___

WEDNESDAY ___/___

THURSDAY ___/___

FRIDAY ___/___

SATURDAY ___/___

OUR GOALS THIS MONTH

Month: _______________________________

Academic:

Spiritual:

Social / Family:

Personal Growth:

Planning / Organizing:

Giving:

Field Trips This Month:

Month: _______________________________________

sunday	monday	tuesday	wednesday

thursday	friday	saturday

Torah Portions

Torah:

Haftorah:

Besora:

Torah:

Haftorah:

Besora:

Torah:

Haftorah:

Besora:

Torah:

Haftorah:

Besora:

Torah:

Haftorah:

Besora:

week of: ___________________________

<table>
<tr><td>word of the week:</td><td>weekly gratitude:</td></tr>
</table>

SCHOOL	SPIRITUAL	MEMORY WORK

THIS WEEKS MENU

S	M	T	W	T	F
B	B	B	B	B	B
L	L	L	L	L	L
D	D	D	D	D	D

SUNDAY ___/___

MONDAY ___/___

TUESDAY ___/___

WEDNESDAY ___/___

THURSDAY ___/___

FRIDAY ___/___

SATURDAY ___/___

word of the week:	weekly gratitude:

SCHOOL   SPIRITUAL   MEMORY WORK

THIS WEEKS MENU

S	M	T	W	T	F	
B	B	B	B	B	B	B
L	L	L	L	L	L	L
D	D	D	D	D	D	D

SUNDAY ___/___

MONDAY ___/___

TUESDAY ___/___

WEDNESDAY ___/___

THURSDAY ___/___

FRIDAY ___/___

SATURDAY ___/___

week of: _______________________

<table>
<tr><td>word of the week:</td><td>weekly gratitude:</td></tr>
</table>

SCHOOL

SPIRITUAL

MEMORY WORK

THIS WEEKS MENU

S	M	T	W	T	F	
B	B	B	B	B	B	B
L	L	L	L	L	L	L
D	D	D	D	D	D	D

SUNDAY ___/___

MONDAY ___/___

TUESDAY ___/___

WEDNESDAY ___/___

THURSDAY ___/___

FRIDAY ___/___

SATURDAY ___/___

week of: _______________________

| word of the week: | weekly gratitude: |

SCHOOL

SPIRITUAL

MEMORY WORK

THIS WEEKS MENU

S	M	T	W	T	F
B	B	B	B	B	B	B
L	L	L	L	L	L	L
D	D	D	D	D	D	D

SUNDAY ____/____

MONDAY ____/____

TUESDAY ____/____

WEDNESDAY ____/____

THURSDAY ____/____

FRIDAY ____/____

SATURDAY ____/____

week of: _______________________________

| word of the week: | weekly gratitude: |

SCHOOL   SPIRITUAL   MEMORY WORK

THIS WEEKS MENU

S	M	T	W	T	F

B	B	B	B	B	B	B
L	L	L	L	L	L	L
D	D	D	D	D	D	D

SUNDAY ___/___

MONDAY ___/___

TUESDAY ___/___

WEDNESDAY ___/___

THURSDAY ___/___

FRIDAY ___/___

SATURDAY ___/___

OUR GOALS THIS MONTH

Month: ______________________________

Academic:

Spiritual:

Social / Family:

Personal Growth:

Planning / Organizing:

Giving:

Field Trips This Month:

sunday	monday	tuesday	wednesday

<table>
<tr><td>thursday</td><td>friday</td><td>saturday</td><td>**Torah Portions**</td></tr>
<tr><td></td><td></td><td></td><td>Torah:

Haftorah:

Besora:</td></tr>
<tr><td></td><td></td><td></td><td>Torah:

Haftorah:

Besora:</td></tr>
<tr><td></td><td></td><td></td><td>Torah:

Haftorah:

Besora:</td></tr>
<tr><td></td><td></td><td></td><td>Torah:

Haftorah:

Besora:</td></tr>
<tr><td></td><td></td><td></td><td>Torah:

Haftorah:

Besora:</td></tr>
</table>

week of: _______________________________________

| word of the week: | weekly gratitude: |

SCHOOL

SPIRITUAL

MEMORY WORK

THIS WEEKS MENU

S	M	T	W	T	F
B	B	B	B	B	B	B
L	L	L	L	L	L	L
D	D	D	D	D	D	D

SUNDAY ___/___

MONDAY ___/___

TUESDAY ___/___

WEDNESDAY ___/___

THURSDAY ___/___

FRIDAY ___/___

SATURDAY ___/___

week of: ________________________

word of the week:	weekly gratitude:

SCHOOL

SPIRITUAL

MEMORY WORK

THIS WEEKS MENU

S	M	T	W	T	F	
B	B	B	B	B	B	B
L	L	L	L	L	L	L
D	D	D	D	D	D	D

SUNDAY ___/___

MONDAY ___/___

TUESDAY ___/___

WEDNESDAY ___/___

THURSDAY ___/___

FRIDAY ___/___

SATURDAY ___/___

THIS WEEKS MENU

SUNDAY ___/___

MONDAY ___/___

TUESDAY ___/___

WEDNESDAY ___/___

THURSDAY ___/___

FRIDAY ___/___

SATURDAY ___/___

week of: ________________

word of the week:	weekly gratitude:

SCHOOL	SPIRITUAL	MEMORY WORK

THIS WEEKS MENU

S	M	T	W	T	F	
B	B	B	B	B	B	B
L	L	L	L	L	L	L
D	D	D	D	D	D	D

SUNDAY ___/___

MONDAY ___/___

TUESDAY ___/___

WEDNESDAY ___/___

THURSDAY ___/___

FRIDAY ___/___

SATURDAY ___/___

week of: _______________________________

word of the week:

weekly gratitude:

SCHOOL

SPIRITUAL

MEMORY WORK

THIS WEEKS MENU

S	M	T	W	T	F
B	B	B	B	B	B	B
L	L	L	L	L	L	L
D	D	D	D	D	D	D

SUNDAY ____/____

MONDAY ____/____

TUESDAY ____/____

WEDNESDAY ____/____

THURSDAY ____/____

FRIDAY ____/____

SATURDAY ____/____

OUR GOALS THIS MONTH

Month: _______________________________

Academic:

Spiritual:

Social / Family:

Personal Growth:

Planning / Organizing:

Giving:

Field Trips This Month:

Month: _______________________________________

sunday	monday	tuesday	wednesday

<table>
<tr><th>thursday</th><th>friday</th><th>saturday</th><th>Torah Portions</th></tr>
<tr><td></td><td></td><td></td><td>Torah:

Haftorah:

Besora:</td></tr>
<tr><td></td><td></td><td></td><td>Torah:

Haftorah:

Besora:</td></tr>
<tr><td></td><td></td><td></td><td>Torah:

Haftorah:

Besora:</td></tr>
<tr><td></td><td></td><td></td><td>Torah:

Haftorah:

Besora:</td></tr>
<tr><td></td><td></td><td></td><td>Torah:

Haftorah:

Besora:</td></tr>
</table>

week of: ____

word of the week:	weekly gratitude:

SCHOOL · SPIRITUAL · MEMORY WORK

THIS WEEKS MENU

S	M	T	W	T	F
B	B	B	B	B	B
L	L	L	L	L	L
D	D	D	D	D	D

SUNDAY ___/___

MONDAY ___/___

TUESDAY ___/___

WEDNESDAY ___/___

THURSDAY ___/___

FRIDAY ___/___

SATURDAY ___/___

week of: ___________________________

<table>
<tr><td>word of the week:</td><td>weekly gratitude:</td></tr>
</table>

SCHOOL   SPIRITUAL   MEMORY WORK

THIS WEEKS MENU

	S	M	T	W	T	F
B						
L						
D						

SUNDAY ___/___

MONDAY ___/___

TUESDAY ___/___

WEDNESDAY ___/___

THURSDAY ___/___

FRIDAY ___/___

SATURDAY ___/___

week of: ___________________________________

word of the week:	weekly gratitude:

SCHOOL	SPIRITUAL	MEMORY WORK

THIS WEEKS MENU

S	M	T	W	T	F	
B	B	B	B	B	B	B
L	L	L	L	L	L	L
D	D	D	D	D	D	D

| SUNDAY ___/___ |
| MONDAY ___/___ |
| TUESDAY ___/___ |
| WEDNESDAY ___/___ |
| THURSDAY ___/___ |
| FRIDAY ___/___ |
| SATURDAY ___/___ |

week of: _______________________

<table>
<tr><td>word of the week:</td><td>weekly gratitude:</td></tr>
</table>

SCHOOL	SPIRITUAL	MEMORY WORK

THIS WEEKS MENU

S	M	T	W	T	F	
B	B	B	B	B	B	B
L	L	L	L	L	L	L
D	D	D	D	D	D	D

SUNDAY ___/___

MONDAY ___/___

TUESDAY ___/___

WEDNESDAY ___/___

THURSDAY ___/___

FRIDAY ___/___

SATURDAY ___/___

week of: _______________________________

| word of the week: | weekly gratitude: |

SCHOOL

SPIRITUAL

MEMORY WORK

THIS WEEKS MENU

	S	M	T	W	T	F
B	B	B	B	B	B	B
L	L	L	L	L	L	L
D	D	D	D	D	D	D

SUNDAY ___/___

MONDAY ___/___

TUESDAY ___/___

WEDNESDAY ___/___

THURSDAY ___/___

FRIDAY ___/___

SATURDAY ___/___

OUR GOALS THIS MONTH

Month: _______________________________

Academic:

Spiritual:

Social / Family:

Personal Growth:

Planning / Organizing:

Giving:

Field Trips This Month:

Month: _______________________________

sunday	monday	tuesday	wednesday

thursday	friday	saturday

Torah Portions

Torah:

Haftorah:

Besora:

Torah:

Haftorah:

Besora:

Torah:

Haftorah:

Besora:

Torah:

Haftorah:

Besora:

Torah:

Haftorah:

Besora:

week of: _______________________

<table>
<tr><td>word of the week:</td><td>weekly gratitude:</td></tr>
</table>

SCHOOL

SPIRITUAL

MEMORY WORK

THIS WEEKS MENU

S	M	T	W	T	F
B	B	B	B	B	B	B
L	L	L	L	L	L	L
D	D	D	D	D	D	D

SUNDAY ____/____

MONDAY ____/____

TUESDAY ____/____

WEDNESDAY ____/____

THURSDAY ____/____

FRIDAY ____/____

SATURDAY ____/____

week of: _______________________

<table>
<tr><td>word of the week:</td><td>weekly gratitude:</td></tr>
</table>

SCHOOL   SPIRITUAL   MEMORY WORK

THIS WEEKS MENU

	S	M	T	W	T	F
B							
L							
D							

SUNDAY ____/____

MONDAY ____/____

TUESDAY ____/____

WEDNESDAY ____/____

THURSDAY ____/____

FRIDAY ____/____

SATURDAY ____/____

week of: ________________

<table>
<tr><td>word of the week:</td><td>weekly gratitude:</td></tr>
</table>

SCHOOL	SPIRITUAL	MEMORY WORK

THIS WEEKS MENU

S	M	T	W	T	F	
B	B	B	B	B	B	B
L	L	L	L	L	L	L
D	D	D	D	D	D	D

SUNDAY ____/____

MONDAY ____/____

TUESDAY ____/____

WEDNESDAY ____/____

THURSDAY ____/____

FRIDAY ____/____

SATURDAY ____/____

week of: _______________________________

<table>
<tr><td>word of the week:</td><td>weekly gratitude:</td></tr>
</table>

SCHOOL	SPIRITUAL	MEMORY WORK

THIS WEEKS MENU

S	M	T	W	T	F	
B	B	B	B	B	B	B
L	L	L	L	L	L	L
D	D	D	D	D	D	D

SUNDAY ____/____

MONDAY ____/____

TUESDAY ____/____

WEDNESDAY ____/____

THURSDAY ____/____

FRIDAY ____/____

SATURDAY ____/____

week of: _______________________________

<table>
<tr><td>word of the week:</td><td>weekly gratitude:</td></tr>
</table>

SCHOOL   SPIRITUAL   MEMORY WORK

THIS WEEKS MENU

S	M	T	W	T	F	
B	B	B	B	B	B	B
L	L	L	L	L	L	L
D	D	D	D	D	D	D

SUNDAY ____/____

MONDAY ____/____

TUESDAY ____/____

WEDNESDAY ____/____

THURSDAY ____/____

FRIDAY ____/____

SATURDAY ____/____

OUR GOALS THIS MONTH

Month: ___________________________

Academic:

Spiritual:

Social / Family:

Personal Growth:

Planning / Organizing:

Giving:

Field Trips This Month:

Month: ____

sunday	monday	tuesday	wednesday

thursday	friday	saturday

Torah Portions

Torah:

Haftorah:

Besora:

Torah:

Haftorah:

Besora:

Torah:

Haftorah:

Besora:

Torah:

Haftorah:

Besora:

Torah:

Haftorah:

Besora:

week of: ___________________________________

<table>
<tr><td>word of the week:</td><td>weekly gratitude:</td></tr>
</table>

SCHOOL   SPIRITUAL   MEMORY WORK

THIS WEEKS MENU

S	M	T	W	T	F
B	B	B	B	B	B
L	L	L	L	L	L
D	D	D	D	D	D

SUNDAY ____/____

MONDAY ____/____

TUESDAY ____/____

WEDNESDAY ____/____

THURSDAY ____/____

FRIDAY ____/____

SATURDAY ____/____

week of: _______________________________

word of the week:	weekly gratitude:

SCHOOL

SPIRITUAL

MEMORY WORK

THIS WEEKS MENU

S	M	T	W	T	F	
B	B	B	B	B	B	B
L	L	L	L	L	L	L
D	D	D	D	D	D	D

SUNDAY ___/___

MONDAY ___/___

TUESDAY ___/___

WEDNESDAY ___/___

THURSDAY ___/___

FRIDAY ___/___

SATURDAY ___/___

Week of: ________________________

<table>
<tr><td>word of the week:</td><td>weekly gratitude:</td></tr>
</table>

SCHOOL	SPIRITUAL	MEMORY WORK

THIS WEEKS MENU

S	M	T	W	T	F	
B	B	B	B	B	B	B
L	L	L	L	L	L	L
D	D	D	D	D	D	D

SUNDAY ___/___

MONDAY ___/___

TUESDAY ___/___

WEDNESDAY ___/___

THURSDAY ___/___

FRIDAY ___/___

SATURDAY ___/___

week of: ________________________________

word of the week:	weekly gratitude:

SCHOOL

SPIRITUAL

MEMORY WORK

THIS WEEKS MENU

S	M	T	W	T	F
B	B	B	B	B	B	B
L	L	L	L	L	L	L
D	D	D	D	D	D	D

SUNDAY ____/____

MONDAY ____/____

TUESDAY ____/____

WEDNESDAY ____/____

THURSDAY ____/____

FRIDAY ____/____

SATURDAY ____/____

week of: _______________________

word of the week:

weekly gratitude:

SCHOOL

SPIRITUAL

MEMORY WORK

THIS WEEKS MENU

S	M	T	W	T	F	
B	B	B	B	B	B	B
L	L	L	L	L	L	L
D	D	D	D	D	D	D

SUNDAY ___/___

MONDAY ___/___

TUESDAY ___/___

WEDNESDAY ___/___

THURSDAY ___/___

FRIDAY ___/___

SATURDAY ___/___

FEAST LESSON PLANNING

FEAST LESSON PLANNING

Feast:

Start Date:

End Date:

Theme / Focus:

Family Planning

Family Traditions/Activities for This Feast:

What We Want to Learn This Year:

Memory Verse for This Feast:

Scripture References for this feast

FEAST WEEK LESSON PLANNING

Feast:

Start Date:

End Date:

Theme / Focus:

Scripture References:

Weekly Lesson & Reflections

Day	Scripture	Activity	Reflection / Notes

FEAST DAILY LESSON PLANNING

Feast:

Date:

Theme / Focus:

Scripture References:

Daily Lesson Planning

Time	Activity	Materials Needed	Notes

FEAST DAILY LESSON PLANNING

Feast:

Date:

Theme / Focus:

Scripture References:

Daily Lesson Planning

Time	Activity	Materials Needed	Notes

FEAST DAILY LESSON PLANNING

Feast:

Date:

Theme / Focus:

Scripture References:

Daily Lesson Planning

Time	Activity	Materials Needed	Notes

FEAST DAILY LESSON PLANNING

Feast:

Date:

Theme / Focus:

Scripture References:

Daily Lesson Planning

Time	Activity	Materials Needed	Notes

FEAST DAILY LESSON PLANNING

Feast:

Date:

Theme / Focus:

Scripture References:

Daily Lesson Planning

Time	Activity	Materials Needed	Notes

FEAST DAILY LESSON PLANNING

Feast:

Date:

Theme / Focus:

Scripture References:

Daily Lesson Planning

Time	Activity	Materials Needed	Notes

FEAST LESSON PLANNING

Feast:

Start Date:

End Date:

Theme / Focus:

Family Planning

Family Traditions/Activities for This Feast:

What We Want to Learn This Year:

Memory Verse for This Feast:

Scripture References for this feast

FEAST WEEK LESSON PLANNING

Feast:

Start Date:

End Date:

Theme / Focus:

Scripture References:

Weekly Lesson & Reflections

Day	Scripture	Activity	Reflection / Notes

FEAST DAILY LESSON PLANNING

Feast:

Date:

Theme / Focus:

Scripture References:

Daily Lesson Planning

Time	Activity	Materials Needed	Notes

FEAST DAILY LESSON PLANNING

Feast:

Date:

Theme / Focus:

Scripture References:

Daily Lesson Planning

Time	Activity	Materials Needed	Notes

FEAST DAILY LESSON PLANNING

Feast:

Date:

Theme / Focus:

Scripture References:

Daily Lesson Planning

Time	Activity	Materials Needed	Notes

FEAST DAILY LESSON PLANNING

Feast:

Date:

Theme / Focus:

Scripture References:

Daily Lesson Planning

Time	Activity	Materials Needed	Notes

FEAST DAILY LESSON PLANNING

Feast:

Date:

Theme / Focus:

Scripture References:

Daily Lesson Planning

Time	Activity	Materials Needed	Notes

FEAST DAILY LESSON PLANNING

Feast:

Date:

Theme / Focus:

Scripture References:

Daily Lesson Planning

Time	Activity	Materials Needed	Notes

FEAST LESSON PLANNING

Feast:

Start Date:

End Date:

Theme / Focus:

Family Planning

Family Traditions/Activities for This Feast:

What We Want to Learn This Year:

Memory Verse for This Feast:

Scripture References for this feast

FEAST WEEK LESSON PLANNING

Feast:

Start Date:

End Date:

Theme / Focus:

Scripture References:

Weekly Lesson & Reflections

Day	Scripture	Activity	Reflection / Notes

FEAST DAILY LESSON PLANNING

Feast:

Date:

Theme / Focus:

Scripture References:

Daily Lesson Planning

Time	Activity	Materials Needed	Notes

FEAST DAILY LESSON PLANNING

Feast:

Date:

Theme / Focus:

Scripture References:

Daily Lesson Planning

Time	Activity	Materials Needed	Notes

FEAST DAILY LESSON PLANNING

Feast:

Date:

Theme / Focus:

Scripture References:

Daily Lesson Planning

Time	Activity	Materials Needed	Notes

FEAST DAILY LESSON PLANNING

Feast:

Date:

Theme / Focus:

Scripture References:

Daily Lesson Planning

Time	Activity	Materials Needed	Notes

FEAST DAILY LESSON PLANNING

Feast:

Date:

Theme / Focus:

Scripture References:

Daily Lesson Planning

Time	Activity	Materials Needed	Notes

FEAST DAILY LESSON PLANNING

Feast:

Date:

Theme / Focus:

Scripture References:

Daily Lesson Planning

Time	Activity	Materials Needed	Notes

FEAST LESSON PLANNING

Feast:

Start Date:

End Date:

Theme / Focus:

Family Planning

Family Traditions/Activities for This Feast:

What We Want to Learn This Year:

Memory Verse for This Feast:

Scripture References for this feast

FEAST WEEK LESSON PLANNING

Feast:

Start Date:

End Date:

Theme / Focus:

Scripture References:

Weekly Lesson & Reflections

Day	Scripture	Activity	Reflection / Notes

FEAST DAILY LESSON PLANNING

Feast:

Date:

Theme / Focus:

Scripture References:

Daily Lesson Planning

Time	Activity	Materials Needed	Notes

FEAST DAILY LESSON PLANNING

Feast:

Date:

Theme / Focus:

Scripture References:

Daily Lesson Planning

Time	Activity	Materials Needed	Notes

FEAST DAILY LESSON PLANNING

Feast:

Date:

Theme / Focus:

Scripture References:

Daily Lesson Planning

Time	Activity	Materials Needed	Notes

FEAST DAILY LESSON PLANNING

Feast:

Date:

Theme / Focus:

Scripture References:

Daily Lesson Planning

Time	Activity	Materials Needed	Notes

FEAST DAILY LESSON PLANNING

Feast:

Date:

Theme / Focus:

Scripture References:

Daily Lesson Planning

Time	Activity	Materials Needed	Notes

FEAST DAILY LESSON PLANNING

Feast:

Date:

Theme / Focus:

Scripture References:

Daily Lesson Planning

Time	Activity	Materials Needed	Notes

FEAST LESSON PLANNING

Feast:

Start Date:

End Date:

Theme / Focus:

Family Planning

Family Traditions/Activities for This Feast:

What We Want to Learn This Year:

Memory Verse for This Feast:

Scripture References for this feast

FEAST WEEK LESSON PLANNING

Feast:

Start Date:

End Date:

Theme / Focus:

Scripture References:

Weekly Lesson & Reflections

Day	Scripture	Activity	Reflection / Notes

FEAST DAILY LESSON PLANNING

Feast:

Date:

Theme / Focus:

Scripture References:

Daily Lesson Planning

Time	Activity	Materials Needed	Notes

FEAST DAILY LESSON PLANNING

Feast:

Date:

Theme / Focus:

Scripture References:

Daily Lesson Planning

Time	Activity	Materials Needed	Notes

FEAST DAILY LESSON PLANNING

Feast:

Date:

Theme / Focus:

Scripture References:

Daily Lesson Planning

Time	Activity	Materials Needed	Notes

FEAST DAILY LESSON PLANNING

Feast:

Date:

Theme / Focus:

Scripture References:

Daily Lesson Planning

Time	Activity	Materials Needed	Notes

FEAST DAILY LESSON PLANNING

Feast:

Date:

Theme / Focus:

Scripture References:

Daily Lesson Planning

Time	Activity	Materials Needed	Notes

FEAST DAILY LESSON PLANNING

Feast:

Date:

Theme / Focus:

Scripture References:

Daily Lesson Planning

Time	Activity	Materials Needed	Notes

FEAST LESSON PLANNING

Feast:

Start Date:

End Date:

Theme / Focus:

Family Planning

Family Traditions/Activities for This Feast:

What We Want to Learn This Year:

Memory Verse for This Feast:

Scripture References for this feast

FEAST WEEK LESSON PLANNING

Feast:

Start Date:

End Date:

Theme / Focus:

Scripture References:

Weekly Lesson & Reflections

Day	Scripture	Activity	Reflection / Notes

FEAST DAILY LESSON PLANNING

Feast:

Date:

Theme / Focus:

Scripture References:

Daily Lesson Planning

Time	Activity	Materials Needed	Notes

FEAST DAILY LESSON PLANNING

Feast:

Date:

Theme / Focus:

Scripture References:

Daily Lesson Planning

Time	Activity	Materials Needed	Notes

FEAST DAILY LESSON PLANNING

Feast:

Date:

Theme / Focus:

Scripture References:

Daily Lesson Planning

Time	Activity	Materials Needed	Notes

FEAST DAILY LESSON PLANNING

Feast:

Date:

Theme / Focus:

Scripture References:

Daily Lesson Planning

Time	Activity	Materials Needed	Notes

FEAST DAILY LESSON PLANNING

Feast:

Date:

Theme / Focus:

Scripture References:

Daily Lesson Planning

Time	Activity	Materials Needed	Notes

FEAST DAILY LESSON PLANNING

Feast:

Date:

Theme / Focus:

Scripture References:

Daily Lesson Planning

Time	Activity	Materials Needed	Notes

FEAST LESSON PLANNING

Feast:

Start Date:

End Date:

Theme / Focus:

Family Planning

Family Traditions/Activities for This Feast:

What We Want to Learn This Year:

Memory Verse for This Feast:

Scripture References for this feast

FEAST WEEK LESSON PLANNING

Feast:

Start Date:

End Date:

Theme / Focus:

Scripture References:

Weekly Lesson & Reflections

Day	Scripture	Activity	Reflection / Notes

FEAST DAILY LESSON PLANNING

Feast:

Date:

Theme / Focus:

Scripture References:

Daily Lesson Planning

Time	Activity	Materials Needed	Notes

FEAST DAILY LESSON PLANNING

Feast:

Date:

Theme / Focus:

Scripture References:

Daily Lesson Planning

Time	Activity	Materials Needed	Notes

FEAST DAILY LESSON PLANNING

Feast:

Date:

Theme / Focus:

Scripture References:

Daily Lesson Planning

Time	Activity	Materials Needed	Notes

FEAST DAILY LESSON PLANNING

Feast:

Date:

Theme / Focus:

Scripture References:

Daily Lesson Planning

Time	Activity	Materials Needed	Notes

FEAST DAILY LESSON PLANNING

Feast:

Date:

Theme / Focus:

Scripture References:

Daily Lesson Planning

Time	Activity	Materials Needed	Notes

FEAST DAILY LESSON PLANNING

Feast:

Date:

Theme / Focus:

Scripture References:

Daily Lesson Planning

Time	Activity	Materials Needed	Notes

EXTRAS

READING LOG

Name: _______________________________

Date	Title	Author	Pages

READING LOG

Name: _______________________________

Date	Title	Author	Pages

READING LOG

Name: _______________________________

Date	Title	Author	Pages

READING LOG

Name: _______________________________________

Date	Title	Author	Pages

FIELD TRIP PLANNING

DATE:

LOCATION ____

ADDRESS ____

CONTACT NAME ____

PHONE NUMBER ____

E-MAIL ADDRESS____

COST: $

DATE:

LOCATION ____

ADDRESS ____

CONTACT NAME ____

PHONE NUMBER ____

E-MAIL ADDRESS____

COST: $

FIELD TRIP PLANNING

DATE:

LOCATION ____

ADDRESS ____

CONTACT NAME ____

PHONE NUMBER ____

E-MAIL ADDRESS____

COST: $

DATE:

LOCATION ____

ADDRESS ____

CONTACT NAME ____

PHONE NUMBER ____

E-MAIL ADDRESS____

COST: $

FIELD TRIP PLANNING

DATE:

LOCATION ____

ADDRESS ____

CONTACT NAME ____

PHONE NUMBER ____

E-MAIL ADDRESS ____

COST: $

DATE:

LOCATION ____

ADDRESS ____

CONTACT NAME ____

PHONE NUMBER ____

E-MAIL ADDRESS ____

COST: $

FIELD TRIP LOG

Date	Destination	Subject Covered	Cost
			$
			$
			$
			$
			$
			$
			$
			$
			$
			$
			$
			$
			$
			$
			$
			$
			$
			$
			$
			$
			$

EXTRACURRICULAR LOG

Name: ______________________________

Activity	Start & End Dates	Frequency	Cost

Name: ______________________________

Activity	Start & End Dates	Frequency	Cost

Name: ______________________________

Activity	Start & End Dates	Frequency	Cost

EXTRACURRICULAR LOG

Name: ____

Activity	Start & End Dates	Frequency	Cost

Name: ____

Activity	Start & End Dates	Frequency	Cost

Name: ____

Activity	Start & End Dates	Frequency	Cost

EXTRACURRICULAR LOG

Name: _______________________________

Activity	Start & End Dates	Frequency	Cost

Name: _______________________________

Activity	Start & End Dates	Frequency	Cost

Name: _______________________________

Activity	Start & End Dates	Frequency	Cost

EXTRACURRICULAR LOG

Name: _______________________________

Activity	Start & End Dates	Frequency	Cost

Name: _______________________________

Activity	Start & End Dates	Frequency	Cost

Name: _______________________________

Activity	Start & End Dates	Frequency	Cost

PROJECT PLANNING

Project Title:

Start Date:

Due Date:

Assigned to:

Goals & Objectives:

Step	Deadline	Done ✔	Materials Needed:

Exra Notes:

PROJECT PLANNING

Project Title:

Start Date:

Due Date:

Assigned to:

Goals & Objectives:

Step	Deadline	Done ✔	Materials Needed:

Exra Notes:

PROJECT PLANNING

Project Title:

Start Date: | Due Date:

Assigned to:

Goals & Objectives:

Step	Deadline	Done ✔	Materials Needed:

Exra Notes:

PROJECT PLANNING

Project Title:

Start Date: | Due Date:

Assigned to:

Goals & Objectives:

Step	Deadline	Done ✔	Materials Needed:

Exra Notes:

GRADE BOOK

Name: _______________________________

Date	Assignment	Grade	Date	Assignment	Grade

GRADE BOOK

Name: _______________________________

Date	Assignment	Grade		Date	Assignment	Grade

GRADE BOOK

Name: ___________________________

Date	Assignment	Grade		Date	Assignment	Grade

GRADE BOOK

Name: _______________________________

Date	Assignment	Grade		Date	Assignment	Grade

GRADE BOOK

Name: _______________________________

Date	Assignment	Grade		Date	Assignment	Grade

GRADE BOOK

Name: _______________________________

Date	Assignment	Grade		Date	Assignment	Grade

Report Card

Name: _______________________________

| Grade Level: | School Year: |

SUBJECTS	1ST	2ND	3RD	4TH

FEED BACK:

Report Card

Name: _______________________

Grade Level:	School Year:

SUBJECTS	1ST	2ND	3RD	4TH

FEED BACK:

Report Card

Name: _______________________________

Grade Level:	School Year:

SUBJECTS	1ST	2ND	3RD	4TH

FEED BACK:

Report Card

Name: ______________________

Grade Level:	School Year:

SUBJECTS	1ST	2ND	3RD	4TH

FEED BACK:

Report Card

Name: ___________________________

Grade Level:	School Year:

SUBJECTS	1ST	2ND	3RD	4TH

FEED BACK:

Report Card

Name: _______________________

| Grade Level: | School Year: |

SUBJECTS	1ST	2ND	3RD	4TH

FEED BACK:

ATTENDANCE

J	F	M	A	M	J	J	A	S	O	N	D
1	1	1	1	1	1	1	1	1	1	1	1
2	2	2	2	2	2	2	2	2	2	2	2
3	3	3	3	3	3	3	3	3	3	3	3
4	4	4	4	4	4	4	4	4	4	4	4
5	5	5	5	5	5	5	5	5	5	5	5
6	6	6	6	6	6	6	6	6	6	6	6
7	7	7	7	7	7	7	7	7	7	7	7
8	8	8	8	8	8	8	8	8	8	8	8
9	9	9	9	9	9	9	9	9	9	9	9
10	10	10	10	10	10	10	10	10	10	10	10
11	11	11	11	11	11	11	11	11	11	11	11
12	12	12	12	12	12	12	12	12	12	12	12
13	13	13	13	13	13	13	13	13	13	13	13
14	14	14	14	14	14	14	14	14	14	14	14
15	15	15	15	15	15	15	15	15	15	15	15
16	16	16	16	16	16	16	16	16	16	16	16
17	17	17	17	17	17	17	17	17	17	17	17
18	18	18	18	18	18	18	18	18	18	18	18
19	19	19	19	19	19	19	19	19	19	19	19
20	20	20	20	20	20	20	20	20	20	20	20
21	21	21	21	21	21	21	21	21	21	21	21
22	22	22	22	22	22	22	22	22	22	22	22
23	23	23	23	23	23	23	23	23	23	23	23
24	24	24	24	24	24	24	24	24	24	24	24
25	25	25	25	25	25	25	25	25	25	25	25
26	26	26	26	26	26	26	26	26	26	26	26
27	27	27	27	27	27	27	27	27	27	27	27
28	28	28	28	28	28	28	28	28	28	28	28
29	29	29	29	29	29	29	29	29	29	29	29
30		30	30	30	30	30	30	30	30	30	30
31		31		31	31		31		31		31

Name:

Grade:

Year:

School Day Counter

January:
February:
March:
April:
May:
June:
July:
August:
September:
October:
November:
December:

Total Days Attended:

Total Days Absent:

ATTENDANCE

J	F	M	A	M	J	J	A	S	O	N	D
1	1	1	1	1	1	1	1	1	1	1	1
2	2	2	2	2	2	2	2	2	2	2	2
3	3	3	3	3	3	3	3	3	3	3	3
4	4	4	4	4	4	4	4	4	4	4	4
5	5	5	5	5	5	5	5	5	5	5	5
6	6	6	6	6	6	6	6	6	6	6	6
7	7	7	7	7	7	7	7	7	7	7	7
8	8	8	8	8	8	8	8	8	8	8	8
9	9	9	9	9	9	9	9	9	9	9	9
10	10	10	10	10	10	10	10	10	10	10	10
11	11	11	11	11	11	11	11	11	11	11	11
12	12	12	12	12	12	12	12	12	12	12	12
13	13	13	13	13	13	13	13	13	13	13	13
14	14	14	14	14	14	14	14	14	14	14	14
15	15	15	15	15	15	15	15	15	15	15	15
16	16	16	16	16	16	16	16	16	16	16	16
17	17	17	17	17	17	17	17	17	17	17	17
18	18	18	18	18	18	18	18	18	18	18	18
19	19	19	19	19	19	19	19	19	19	19	19
20	20	20	20	20	20	20	20	20	20	20	20
21	21	21	21	21	21	21	21	21	21	21	21
22	22	22	22	22	22	22	22	22	22	22	22
23	23	23	23	23	23	23	23	23	23	23	23
24	24	24	24	24	24	24	24	24	24	24	24
25	25	25	25	25	25	25	25	25	25	25	25
26	26	26	26	26	26	26	26	26	26	26	26
27	27	27	27	27	27	27	27	27	27	27	27
28	28	28	28	28	28	28	28	28	28	28	28
29	29	29	29	29	29	29	29	29	29	29	29
30		30	30	30	30	30	30	30	30	30	30
31		31		31	31		31		31		31

Name:

Grade:

Year:

School Day Counter

| January: |
| February: |
| March: |
| April: |
| May: |
| June: |
| July: |
| August: |
| September: |
| October: |
| November: |
| December: |

Total Days Attended:

Total Days Absent:

ATTENDANCE

J	F	M	A	M	J	J	A	S	O	N	D
1	1	1	1	1	1	1	1	1	1	1	1
2	2	2	2	2	2	2	2	2	2	2	2
3	3	3	3	3	3	3	3	3	3	3	3
4	4	4	4	4	4	4	4	4	4	4	4
5	5	5	5	5	5	5	5	5	5	5	5
6	6	6	6	6	6	6	6	6	6	6	6
7	7	7	7	7	7	7	7	7	7	7	7
8	8	8	8	8	8	8	8	8	8	8	8
9	9	9	9	9	9	9	9	9	9	9	9
10	10	10	10	10	10	10	10	10	10	10	10
11	11	11	11	11	11	11	11	11	11	11	11
12	12	12	12	12	12	12	12	12	12	12	12
13	13	13	13	13	13	13	13	13	13	13	13
14	14	14	14	14	14	14	14	14	14	14	14
15	15	15	15	15	15	15	15	15	15	15	15
16	16	16	16	16	16	16	16	16	16	16	16
17	17	17	17	17	17	17	17	17	17	17	17
18	18	18	18	18	18	18	18	18	18	18	18
19	19	19	19	19	19	19	19	19	19	19	19
20	20	20	20	20	20	20	20	20	20	20	20
21	21	21	21	21	21	21	21	21	21	21	21
22	22	22	22	22	22	22	22	22	22	22	22
23	23	23	23	23	23	23	23	23	23	23	23
24	24	24	24	24	24	24	24	24	24	24	24
25	25	25	25	25	25	25	25	25	25	25	25
26	26	26	26	26	26	26	26	26	26	26	26
27	27	27	27	27	27	27	27	27	27	27	27
28	28	28	28	28	28	28	28	28	28	28	28
29	29	29	29	29	29	29	29	29	29	29	29
30		30	30	30	30	30	30	30	30	30	30
31		31		31	31		31		31		31

Name:

Grade:

Year:

School Day Counter

January:

February:

March:

April:

May:

June:

July:

August:

September:

October:

November:

December:

Total Days Attended:

Total Days Absent:

ATTENDANCE

J	F	M	A	M	J	J	A	S	O	N	D
1	1	1	1	1	1	1	1	1	1	1	1
2	2	2	2	2	2	2	2	2	2	2	2
3	3	3	3	3	3	3	3	3	3	3	3
4	4	4	4	4	4	4	4	4	4	4	4
5	5	5	5	5	5	5	5	5	5	5	5
6	6	6	6	6	6	6	6	6	6	6	6
7	7	7	7	7	7	7	7	7	7	7	7
8	8	8	8	8	8	8	8	8	8	8	8
9	9	9	9	9	9	9	9	9	9	9	9
10	10	10	10	10	10	10	10	10	10	10	10
11	11	11	11	11	11	11	11	11	11	11	11
12	12	12	12	12	12	12	12	12	12	12	12
13	13	13	13	13	13	13	13	13	13	13	13
14	14	14	14	14	14	14	14	14	14	14	14
15	15	15	15	15	15	15	15	15	15	15	15
16	16	16	16	16	16	16	16	16	16	16	16
17	17	17	17	17	17	17	17	17	17	17	17
18	18	18	18	18	18	18	18	18	18	18	18
19	19	19	19	19	19	19	19	19	19	19	19
20	20	20	20	20	20	20	20	20	20	20	20
21	21	21	21	21	21	21	21	21	21	21	21
22	22	22	22	22	22	22	22	22	22	22	22
23	23	23	23	23	23	23	23	23	23	23	23
24	24	24	24	24	24	24	24	24	24	24	24
25	25	25	25	25	25	25	25	25	25	25	25
26	26	26	26	26	26	26	26	26	26	26	26
27	27	27	27	27	27	27	27	27	27	27	27
28	28	28	28	28	28	28	28	28	28	28	28
29	29	29	29	29	29	29	29	29	29	29	29
30		30	30	30	30	30	30	30	30	30	30
31		31		31		31	31		31		31

Name:

Grade:

Year:

School Day Counter

January:
February:
March:
April:
May:
June:
July:
August:
September:
October:
November:
December:

Total Days Attended:
Total Days Absent:

ATTENDANCE

J	F	M	A	M	J	J	A	S	O	N	D
1	1	1	1	1	1	1	1	1	1	1	1
2	2	2	2	2	2	2	2	2	2	2	2
3	3	3	3	3	3	3	3	3	3	3	3
4	4	4	4	4	4	4	4	4	4	4	4
5	5	5	5	5	5	5	5	5	5	5	5
6	6	6	6	6	6	6	6	6	6	6	6
7	7	7	7	7	7	7	7	7	7	7	7
8	8	8	8	8	8	8	8	8	8	8	8
9	9	9	9	9	9	9	9	9	9	9	9
10	10	10	10	10	10	10	10	10	10	10	10
11	11	11	11	11	11	11	11	11	11	11	11
12	12	12	12	12	12	12	12	12	12	12	12
13	13	13	13	13	13	13	13	13	13	13	13
14	14	14	14	14	14	14	14	14	14	14	14
15	15	15	15	15	15	15	15	15	15	15	15
16	16	16	16	16	16	16	16	16	16	16	16
17	17	17	17	17	17	17	17	17	17	17	17
18	18	18	18	18	18	18	18	18	18	18	18
19	19	19	19	19	19	19	19	19	19	19	19
20	20	20	20	20	20	20	20	20	20	20	20
21	21	21	21	21	21	21	21	21	21	21	21
22	22	22	22	22	22	22	22	22	22	22	22
23	23	23	23	23	23	23	23	23	23	23	23
24	24	24	24	24	24	24	24	24	24	24	24
25	25	25	25	25	25	25	25	25	25	25	25
26	26	26	26	26	26	26	26	26	26	26	26
27	27	27	27	27	27	27	27	27	27	27	27
28	28	28	28	28	28	28	28	28	28	28	28
29	29	29	29	29	29	29	29	29	29	29	29
30		30	30	30	30	30	30	30	30	30	30
31		31		31	31		31		31		31

Name:

Grade:

Year:

School Day Counter

January:	
February:	
March:	
April:	
May:	
June:	
July:	
August:	
September:	
October:	
November:	
December:	

Total Days Attended:

Total Days Absent:

ATTENDANCE

J F M A M J J A S O N D

1	1	1	1	1	1	1	1	1	1	1	1
2	2	2	2	2	2	2	2	2	2	2	2
3	3	3	3	3	3	3	3	3	3	3	3
4	4	4	4	4	4	4	4	4	4	4	4
5	5	5	5	5	5	5	5	5	5	5	5
6	6	6	6	6	6	6	6	6	6	6	6
7	7	7	7	7	7	7	7	7	7	7	7
8	8	8	8	8	8	8	8	8	8	8	8
9	9	9	9	9	9	9	9	9	9	9	9
10	10	10	10	10	10	10	10	10	10	10	10
11	11	11	11	11	11	11	11	11	11	11	11
12	12	12	12	12	12	12	12	12	12	12	12
13	13	13	13	13	13	13	13	13	13	13	13
14	14	14	14	14	14	14	14	14	14	14	14
15	15	15	15	15	15	15	15	15	15	15	15
16	16	16	16	16	16	16	16	16	16	16	16
17	17	17	17	17	17	17	17	17	17	17	17
18	18	18	18	18	18	18	18	18	18	18	18
19	19	19	19	19	19	19	19	19	19	19	19
20	20	20	20	20	20	20	20	20	20	20	20
21	21	21	21	21	21	21	21	21	21	21	21
22	22	22	22	22	22	22	22	22	22	22	22
23	23	23	23	23	23	23	23	23	23	23	23
24	24	24	24	24	24	24	24	24	24	24	24
25	25	25	25	25	25	25	25	25	25	25	25
26	26	26	26	26	26	26	26	26	26	26	26
27	27	27	27	27	27	27	27	27	27	27	27
28	28	28	28	28	28	28	28	28	28	28	28
29	29	29	29	29	29	29	29	29	29	29	29
30		30	30	30	30	30	30	30	30	30	30
31		31		31	31		31		31		31

Name:

Grade:

Year:

School Day Counter

January:

February:

March:

April:

May:

June:

July:

August:

September:

October:

November:

December:

Total Days Attended:

Total Days Absent: